GRACE IN THE WOUND

GRACE IN THE WOUND

Finding Hope in Long-Term Grief

KATHY HENDRICKS

twentythirdpublications.com

TWENTY-THIRD PUBLICATIONS
977 Hartford Turnpike Unit A
Waterford, CT 06385
(860) 437-3012 or (800) 321-0411
www.twentythirdpublications.com

Copyright © 2023 Kathy Hendricks. All rights reserved. No part of this publication may be reproduced in any manner without prior written permission of the publisher. Write to the Permissions Editor.

Scripture texts in this work are taken from the New American Bible, revised edition © 2010, 1991, 1986, 1970 Confraternity of Christian Doctrine, Washington, D.C. and are used by permission of the copyright owner. All Rights Reserved. No part of the New American Bible may be reproduced in any form without permission in writing from the copyright owner.

Cover photo: stock.adobe.com/Jorm S

ISBN: 978-1-62785-740-6
Printed in the U.S.A.

 A division of Bayard, Inc.

For my grandchildren
*Toni, River,
and Clay*

Contents

Introduction 1

Jenny's Story 4

ONE
The Awful Grace of God 9

TWO
When Heart Meets Heart
Moving Beyond Unacknowledged Grief 21

THREE
From Transmittal to Transformation
Unresolved Grief 41

FOUR
Mellowness of Heart
The Long View 59

FIVE
The Grace in Grief 73

Resources 86

INTRODUCTION

"Blessed are they who mourn, for they will be comforted." MATTHEW 5:4

It has been over four decades since I cradled my first child. Jenny was just past a year old when we found her lifeless body in her crib. While the immediate aftermath and resultant process of bereavement is long past, the grief is still there. The years have mellowed the piercing sadness and longing for her, but now and then the heart wound opens again. The trigger might be a photograph, the sight of a child with Down syndrome, or the passing of yet another anniversary. "Closure" is neither possible nor desired.

There is no shortage of books on grieving, but most are limited to the immediate period following a death. The topic of grief is often confined to the first year or two, and therefore these books carry an unintentional message that bereavement is over and done with. Those walking the path of long-term grief know this to be a fallacy. One doesn't simply "get over" the death of a beloved child, spouse, parent, sibling, or friend. Other losses factor into this as well. Mourning the demise of one's health, home, job, mobility, or lifelong dream also entails a lengthy process of re-forming one's life and moving forward. The adage "time heals all wounds" puts no constraints around *how much* time is needed. Even so, our culture has little tolerance for heartbreak. We tend to streamline the process and sometimes limit it to a couple of hours a week in a support group. While these gatherings offer a vital way of helping people through the process, grief cannot be confined to a particular meeting place or timeline. Author Mirabai Starr describes it beautifully:

> There is no map for the landscape of loss, no established itinerary, no cosmic checklist, where each item ticked off gets you closer to success. You cannot *succeed* in mourning your loved ones. You cannot fail. Nor is grief a malady, like the flu. You will not get over it. You will only come to integrate your loss…The death of a beloved is an amputation. You find a new center of gravity, but the limb does not grow back. (*Caravan of No Despair: A Memoir of Loss and Transformation*)

Just as there are few resources about grieving over a long period of time, it is difficult to find ones that address the grace that can emerge from the experience. This book addresses both. The first chapter begins with a recognition of grace and the mysterious way in which it might emanate from the deepest wounds. In chapters 2 and 3, I explore the devastating effects of unacknowledged and unresolved grief and the long-range effects on one's life. The fourth chapter considers ways in which the heart

Introduction

grows mellow as a result of long-term grief—something that comes in a gradual fashion by befriending our woundedness and integrating it into our lives. The book concludes by circling around to the meaning of grace and the movement forward through gratitude, openness, and hope—not as a way to put grief behind us but to see how it opens up into something truly heavenly and generative. Each chapter begins with a passage from one of the post-Resurrection accounts in the Gospels. These help to illuminate various ways of finding God's grace in our grief and allowing it to draw forth new life. Questions at various points in each chapter can be used for individual reflection or conversation with others.

I am well aware of the danger of funneling a topic as large as grief through one's personal story. Nevertheless, my experience of grieving Jenny's death for over forty years serves as a backdrop for the larger themes within each chapter. Therefore, to orient the reader to some of the references made to her short life and the aftermath of her death, I start with her story—and mine. Since you have probably picked up this book because of your own experience, I hope this will serve as an invitation and encouragement to reflect upon and share your own story with someone else.

JENNY'S STORY

July, 1977. Ron and I had been married less than a year, and I was close to giving birth to our first child. We were stationed for a brief period in North Carolina, where Ron was taking a five-month course in airline mechanics. Shortly after the baby's arrival, he would receive his orders from the U.S. Coast Guard to transfer elsewhere. This uncertainty, coupled with the distance from our families and friends, made for an anxious time. Even so, neither of us gave much thought to anything going awry. The day of Jenny's birth was one of wonder and joy mixed with exhaustion and relief. The next day, a doctor entered my room and told me that Jenny had Down syndrome. At that time, the term was not widely used; I had no idea what it meant. Shortly afterward, a nurse brought Jenny back to my room from the nursery. I examined her with a renewed sense of awe. She was tiny and beautiful and seemed perfectly healthy. When Ron came to visit later in the day (even fathers were restricted to specific hours at the time), I tried to relay the doctor's news. While neither of us knew what this meant—for her and for us—we gave thanks for the way in which we had been blessed.

The first sign that something else was wrong came when Jenny struggled to breastfeed. Giving her a bottle of formula caused her to vomit in a violent and frightening manner. Thus began the first round of doctor and hospital visits. By the time Ron received his orders to report to a new air station in Sitka, Alaska, I was able to breastfeed her, thanks to a nurse's helpful guidance. We packed up and started the long journey across the country, stopping along the way to visit my family in Denver. My mother, concerned about Jenny's diagnosis, made an appointment with my sister's pediatrician. He immediately sent us to Children's Hospital. After hours of consultation with various doctors, a surgeon told us she had an intestinal disorder called Hirschsprung's Disease. He explained the need for a colostomy—another unfamiliar term—as a way to help her bowels to function. He went on to tell us that after she reached twenty pounds, her intestine would develop enough to allow for closing the colostomy.

The next several months in Sitka were idyllic. We loved the town and the beauty of our surroundings. The social worker at Children's Hospital contacted a public health nurse who greeted us upon our arrival and introduced us to other parents of children with special needs. Jenny thrived and developed a sweet disposition that endeared her to everyone who met her. We managed the care of her colostomy, albeit with a few challenges, and looked forward to a return to Denver for the follow-up surgery. When that time arrived I took her by myself, as Ron had already used up his leave time to deal with her surgery and the unexpected death of his father soon after our arrival in Alaska. I looked forward to time with my family and to seeing Jenny gain more strength and well-being.

At first, all went as planned. After a day or two, however, she began to grow listless and was in obvious pain. The doctors discovered an infection and took her back into surgery—this time to perform a temporary ileostomy. I spent many anxious days by her bedside, praying that all would be well. Only then did the chief surgeon tell me that a mistake had been made on the original pathology report. Technically, the colostomy should not have worked all those months. Given the outcome, he felt that she had developed enough stamina to go through with the original closure—something that would improve her quality of life. After consulting with Ron, we agreed to this third surgical procedure within a month. She came through like a trooper and, after a couple of weeks' recovery, we were given the okay to return to Sitka.

All was well until she once again grew listless and distressed. I began making daily trips to the public health hospital and begged the doctor to do something to help her. After consultation with her surgeon, it was decided that she needed to return to Denver for treatment. On the morning of our scheduled departure, we found that she had died during the night. While the cause of death was never definitively determined, her doctors suspected peritonitis (inflammation of the tissues lining the abdomen). Her internal organs had sustained massive scarring because of multiple surgeries. This, in turn, could have led to a perforation in her intestine. I was also told that the beneficial aspects of breast milk enabled her to live and to thrive for over a year. While I was left with lots of questions about her life and death, this piece of information brought consolation as my grieving process began.

For Reflection *or* Conversation

What has been your experience of personal loss?

How have you known grief over the long term?

One

The Awful Grace of God

Jesus said to her, "Woman, why are you weeping? Whom are you looking for?" She thought it was the gardener and said to him, "Sir, if you carried him away, tell me where you laid him, and I will take him." Jesus said to her, "Mary!" She turned and said to him in Hebrew, "Rabbouni," which means Teacher. Jesus said to her, "Stop holding on to me, for I have not yet ascended to the Father. But go to my brothers and tell them, 'I am going to my Father and your Father, to my God and your God.'" JOHN 20:15-17

On the morning of my scheduled return to Denver with Jenny, I awoke with a prayer for strength running through my mind. The thought of her undergoing even more surgery was terrifying. After the roller-coaster year with her, I wasn't sure of my own capacity to handle additional hospital vigils or to absorb the worry and strain of watching her try to recover. Her little body had already endured so much. How, I wondered, could she sustain yet another operation? As devastating as it was, her death at home rather than in a hospital was a grace.

TURNING CORNERS

The account of Mary Magdalene's encounter with Jesus in the garden is both tender and jarring. She had witnessed a horrific execution and the dashing of hope. No wonder her first inclination upon recognizing Jesus was to hold onto him. In telling her not to cling to him, wasn't Jesus being a bit cold-hearted?

After years of processing Jenny's death, I can better understand this passage and why it is so vital to let go of the past. Yet, this isn't a quick and easy process. After Jenny died, I had a recurring dream about leaving her in the hospital or forgetting to care for her. At times, I awoke sobbing and shaken by the very thought of being so careless and neglectful. This lasted for several years, until the night when she told me she forgave me. I never had the dream again. In my waking hours, I could recognize the irrational nature of my guilt and remorse. Perhaps, in her own way, Jenny was urging me to let go of whatever restrained me from living more freely. Was this what Jesus did with Mary Magdalene?

My other two children—both born after Jenny's death—moved me farther along in this process. Ron, a gifted photographer, took dozens of pictures of all three children when they were babies. These were pre-digital days, so we had to wait for his photos to be returned, usually as slides. One night he set up the projector and we viewed the pictures in chronological order. In one, Jenny was propped up on the couch at about the age of six months. Her pudgy feet poked out of a pair of sweatpants, and her freshly washed hair stuck straight up, illuminated by the sun streaming through the window behind her. The image brought a tug to my heart until Eric and Anna burst out laughing. It came as a shock and even struck me as irreverent. I took a second look and then relaxed into a smile. What my children saw was an adorable baby and not a tragic figure. For the first time since her death, I recognized her in the same way. I also realized that I needn't be frozen in time as the grieving mother. It was an important turning point—a moment of grace.

DROPLETS OF GRACE

Amazing grace, how sweet the sound…
JOHN NEWTON

As a child, I visualized grace as a milky white substance that cleansed the stain of sin. This arose from a lesson out of the *Baltimore Catechism*—one with an image of the soul as a milk bottle in which varying levels of sanctifying grace displaced each of our sins. Over time, the image matured. Thus, like the "amazing grace" described in John Newton's hymn, I "hear" grace and recognize its profound reverberations in my life. Author Anne Lamott describes it as "a ribbon of mountain air that manages to get through the cracks" (*Grace (Eventually): Thoughts on Faith*). This image makes *breathing* grace even more potent. Rather than rising and falling according to our behavior patterns, grace surrounds us, able to penetrate every pore and vessel. As Newton's lyrics note, it is only by being cracked and broken that we understand its redemptive nature and profound ability to heal and restore life.

The image of the milk bottle stuck with me over the years, perhaps because it was so visual. I could connect with it as a child. It took longer to understand that the container could remain empty for a lengthy period and that much of the grace would come in the form of teardrops—those shed and those withheld. Grace in this context is not always amazing.

> *He who learns must suffer. And even in our sleep pain that cannot forget, falls drop by drop upon the heart, and in our own despair, against our will, comes wisdom to us by the awful grace of God.* AESCHYLUS

This quote by the ancient Greek dramatist Aeschylus helped draw the late Robert F. Kennedy through a devastating experience of loss. The words are engraved in a monument by RFK's own grave and provide a glimpse into both the devastation and the transformation he experienced after the assassination of his brother, President John F. Kennedy. It might seem contradictory to find consolation in the words of "the father of tragedy," as Aeschylus is called, but it makes sense while in the midst of grief. Anyone who experiences the pain that even sleep cannot alleviate can also appreciate the slow drip upon the heart that occurs over the long term. It also leads, over time, to the grace that can emerge through awful events and circumstances.

This is not to say that God sends these losses and trials to test our faith or measure our mettle. I long ago rejected the notion that Jenny's death was part of a divine plan or that God needed another "angel in heaven." Both explanations were offered to me by well-meaning people who didn't know what to say in the wake of my loss. Ironically, it was through the last days of her life and then her death that I came to recognize the God who weeps with us amid our pain and suffering.

Over the years, I also began to understand the value placed upon tears in both the Jewish and Christian traditions. *Penthos* is an ancient Greek word meaning sorrow, grief, or sadness. In both the Hebrew and Christian scriptures, it is associated with contrition or a turning of one's heart away from sin and toward God. Thus, the tears that flow from *penthos* are sacred because of their transformative possibilities. The great mystic Catherine of Siena described the evolving nature of tears that flow first from a punctured heart and, in time, provide an opening to inner growth and eventual consolation from a God of endless love. This is not an overnight process, however. It entails an inner knowing that can only come from suffering.

Another lesson I absorbed as a child—one not as warmly embraced as that of milk bottles full of grace—was that suffering was not only necessary in life but also desired. Here, too, it took some maturation to distinguish redemptive suffering from extreme asceticism. My Catholic upbringing included exposure to the prominence of the cross in Christian tradition. It was a constant presence as part of liturgical rituals, particularly during Lent. At first glance, the veneration of the cross, which takes place during the Good Friday liturgy, seems maudlin and even a bit sadistic. After traversing the long and painful path of loss, however, it becomes possible to recognize "the awful grace of God" enfolded in the practice. More than one saint prayed for a cross that would overcome their pride and school them in humility. While sometimes taken to extremes, such a petition acknowledges the paradoxical nature of human suffering. James Finley, a clinical psychologist and author of several books on contemplation and spirituality, frames it this way: "The deeper the brokenness, the greater the momentum of the descent. The greater the momentum of the descent, the more deeply compassionate love descends into the innermost recesses of our doubts and fears. Suddenly encountering such love, our doubts and fears melt in the love that sets us free" (*Christian Meditation: Experiencing the Presence of God*).

It took a lot longer than one night of viewing baby pictures for me to cease clinging to my grief. As Finley notes, there is a descent that comes with suffering, and it is not reconciled in a single experience. Instead, the grace comes in a drop-by-drop measure that allows us to give voice to our anguish and acknowledge the depth of our pain.

For Reflection *or* Conversation

What is your image of grace?

How have you experienced "the awful grace of God"?

What released you from a hold on past grief?

THE PRAYER OF LAMENT

> *Save me, God, for the waters*
> *have reached my neck.*
> *I have sunk into the mire of the deep,*
> *where there is no foothold.*
> *I have gone down to the watery depths;*
> *the flood overwhelms me.*
> *I am weary with crying out;*
> *my throat is parched.*
> *My eyes fail, from looking for my God.*
>
> PSALM 69:2–4

Those who know the experience of deep and devastating loss can relate to the stark images in Psalm 69: the feeling of being sucked under or pounded by waves of despair, confusion, sadness, or remorse. The strain, exhaustion, parched throat, and strained eyesight that seeks endlessly for consolation from a seemingly absent God. Psalms and other expressions of lament in the Bible don't shortchange the pain of suffering. Such prayers are not an exercise in sentimental hope but an immersion into mystical hope—that for which there are no quick-fix solutions in desperate times. There is no joyful entry into the quicksand of loss.

"How long?" psalms express the desperation that comes with sinking into an abyss of grief. Many of them lament the agonizing silence that makes desperation even more difficult.

> *To you, Lord, I call;*
> *my Rock, do not be deaf to me,*
> *Do not be silent toward me,*
> *so that I join those who go down to the pit.*
> PSALM 28:1

> *You see this, Lord; do not be silent;*
> *Lord, do not withdraw from me.*
> PSALM 35:22

Psalms of desperation wrestle with the "dark night" experiences—those in which the way is uneven and unclear, God is silent and aloof, and all seems lost and forlorn. One of the most difficult things about such experiences is the *waiting*. It is worsened by fears of what could be or by doubt that anything good will come forth. God is silent. In some of these passages, the anguish gives rise to accusations over such indifference.

> *Why, God, have you cast us off forever?*
> *Why does your anger burn against the*
> *sheep of your pasture?* PSALM 74:1

The railing at God amid these prayers might seem sacrilegious when it is, in fact, a testament to faith and endurance. Many of the biblical prayers of lament were composed during times of exile in which the people were cut off from everything comforting, familiar, promising, and secure. Isn't this the experience of loss? We are left disoriented, rootless, and desperate for help. The effects of such loss don't diminish with time or repetition. Having gone through one death won't prepare us for or mitigate the pain of the next one. The death of one's beloved is akin to an amputation. A part of us has been cut away; the loss is permanent even as the immediate aftermath subsides. One of my friends described it as being "ambushed by grief"—an experience she had for years after the death of her husband.

Modern psychology offers a valuable understanding of the way in which grief unfolds. By now, many of us are familiar with the five "stages" of grief: anger, denial, bargaining, depression, and acceptance. We may also understand the danger of getting stuck in one or more of the preliminary stages and thus unable to move to a point of acceptance. While identifying the various aspects of grief is extremely helpful, naming them as stages can give the impression that we move neatly from one to the next. Grief counselors and others steeped in knowledge of bereavement are quick to point out the unevenness of the process. There is no set time frame around any of these movements, nor is there a definitive direction to them. Thus, it is easy to be ambushed by feelings of sadness, loneliness, or desolation well past the first, second, or third year.

The only way *out* of the wilderness, then, is *through* it. As the people of the Exodus discovered, there is no short and straight path from one side to the other. The journey through darkness may be a place of deep encounter with God, one that brings challenge rather than comfort. As the poet T.S. Eliot wrote in "Wait Without Hope," "The faith and the hope and the love are all in the waiting." As we traverse it, we begin to discover the blessings enfolded in the pain. Grace comes in awe-filled ways, and we gradually learn to give ourselves to it. We allow ourselves to let go.

LETTING GO

Our friend Liz crocheted a beautiful white blanket for Jenny when she was born. On the morning of her death, I wrapped it around her body before racing to the hospital—a journey that was quicker than waiting for an ambulance. The blanket, along with her nightclothes, were later retrieved by a fellow parishioner who washed them and returned them to me. The blanket rests on a chair in our bedroom, providing as much warmth and comfort now as it did when Jenny was alive.

We might view grace in this same way. It provides the comfort and consolation we need to overlay our devastation and loss. Rather than stifling the pain, it provides moments of respite and invites us to wrap ourselves within its protective care. "He who learns must suffer," Aeschylus wrote. It's a brutal lesson of life. The death of one's child, spouse, partner, parent, sibling, or dear friend is certainly one of the hardest forms of suffering. With openness, we come to know the grace that falls "drop by drop" into our wounded hearts. Extensions of kindness, thoughtfulness, and compassion ease the immediate ache and provide consolation. I experienced this through the simple gesture of someone returning Jenny's blanket and sleeper—freshly washed and tenderly folded. Over the years, the memory of this and other gestures helped release my grip on the most painful associations with Jenny's last days. I was then free to embrace these extensions of love and compassion and recognize how they drew me through the initial stages of grief.

In the gospel accounts of Jesus' death and burial, Mary Magdalene does not bear her grief alone. She is one of a group of women who mourn together. When Jesus sends her forth to tell others about the Resurrection, we can imagine that she shared her good news not only with the male apostles, but also with the women with whom she experienced so much sorrow and now so much joy. No doubt they continued to support one another as a new phase in their lives began—one that comes when one grieving heart meets another.

For Reflection *or* Conversation

When and how have you been "ambushed by grief"?

Who or what helped you to release your grip on the initial pain of your loss?

How have you continued to let go as your grief has extended over the long term?

Two
When Heart Meets Heart

Moving Beyond Unacknowledged Grief

> *Thomas, called Didymus, one of the Twelve, was not with them when Jesus came. So the other disciples said to him, "We have seen the Lord." But he said to them, "Unless I see the mark of the nails in his hands and put my finger into the nailmarks and put my hand into his side, I will not believe." Now a week later his disciples were again inside and Thomas was with them. Jesus came, although the doors were locked, and stood in their midst and said, "Peace be with you." Then he said to Thomas, "Put your finger here and see my hands, and bring your hand and put it into my side, and do not be unbelieving, but believe." Thomas answered and said to him, "My Lord and my God!"* JOHN 20:24-28

This account from John's gospel had the unfortunate effect of labeling the disciple Thomas as forever "doubting." Viewed from the perspective of one who knows the devastation of deep loss and disillusionment, Thomas' reaction makes sense. Why gets your hopes up when they are likely to be dashed? Rather than chastising Thomas, Jesus invites him to enter his wounds and therein find hope and assurance.

Twelve years after Jenny's death, I underwent another form of bereavement when I had a miscarriage. This was a different form of infant loss, as there were no mementos—no pictures or memories to draw upon for comfort. I soon began receiving condolences from women who had suffered the same loss. It was stunning. They came from friends I had known for over a decade but who had never mentioned their experience. A few years later, I took a job in publishing that entailed the oversight of ministerial resources for women affected by various forms of infant loss: miscarriage, SIDS, stillbirth, and infertility. It brought me in touch with women across the country and overseas who had never shared their stories with others. Presentations on program materials quickly morphed into sharing sessions. Tears flowed freely as heart-to-heart exchanges took place. For some, it was the first time they were able to recall their experience and share their grief. As I listened to the women's stories, I discovered how rarely they found any form of support or care. Instead, there was an unspoken sense that they simply needed to put the whole thing behind them and, as one person told me, "try again."

These experiences provided an initial look at various forms of unacknowledged grief and the toll it takes over the long term. Once attuned to this reality, I began to consider other forms of grief that are unacknowledged or remain hidden. Deaths by suicide in which families carry their grief in isolation, remorse, guilt, and endless questions. The ache of grandparents who have been cut off from their grandchildren due to an acrimonious divorce or alienation from their adult children. Those left behind by people with HIV/AIDS who died alone or who were cut off by fear and misinformation from their family members, spouses, lovers, and friends. As I write this, the death rate from the Covid-19 pandemic has surpassed the one million mark in the U.S. Worldwide, the number tops six million. The aftermath of such loss will take decades to surface and then to be acknowledged by ourselves and others.

In her book *Grief: Contemporary Theory and the Practice of Ministry*, Melissa M. Kelley uses the term "disenfranchised grief" to describe that which lacks social validation or public acknowledgment. This isn't a willful dismissal of grief but often results from misunderstanding the depth of a painful loss or not recognizing the ongoing need for support. I had a touching experience of speaking to women about infant loss at a U.S. military installation in Germany during the 2003 Gulf War. When the topic of miscarriage arose, the women told me it wasn't considered serious enough to warrant bringing a husband back to the base from the front. Thus, the women carried their grief alone or relied on each other for support. The statistics are daunting: 10 to 15 percent of pregnancies end in miscarriage. Since the majority of these happen during the first trimester, women are often left to work through the loss by themselves. In my own case, even though I was working for a Catholic diocese at the time, my parish provided no outreach. As I spoke to individuals and groups of women, this proved to be the norm.

Kelley also notes that the circumstances around a death may cause those who are grieving to refrain from disclosing the facts about their loss out of fear of being judged or stigmatized. A recent example bears this out. As Covid deaths multiplied during the pandemic, so, too, did the number of those grieving the loss of loved ones. In just two years, it became the third leading cause of death in the United States. The sense of community that characterized the early days of the pandemic succumbed to a national sense of ennui around the mind-numbing statistics and then to questions around whether the deceased had been vaccinated. "The pandemic has replaced community with isolation, empathy with judgment, and opportunities for healing with relentless triggers…It has opened up private grief to public scrutiny, all while depriving grievers of the collective support they need to recover. The U.S. seems intent on brushing aside its losses in its desire to move past the crisis. But the grief of millions of people is not going away" (Ed Yong, "The Final Pandemic Betrayal," *The Atlantic*, April 13, 2022). Added to this exclusion is the way in which many people were unable to be with loved ones when they died. Given the quarantines in place, they relied on compassionate nurses and other medical staff who passed along final messages and provided consolation to those dying and those mourning their passing. To make it even worse, funerals were delayed or restricted by social distancing and masking. Only in time will we uncover the massive toll this is taking on our individual and collective psyches.

AVOIDANCE AND DENIAL

As noted in the last chapter, denial is one of the stages of grief and a common response to a deep loss. It becomes a form of disenfranchised grief when it lingers and is magnified by avoidance. A month or two after Jenny's death, I met Mary, a woman whose eleven-year-old daughter was killed by a speeding car while she was riding her bike. The accident had taken place over twenty years earlier. Over that span of time, Mary's husband banned all mention of the girl's name in the family. Perhaps it was knowing how my own heart was shattered by death that spurred Mary to tell her story to me and to a few other women at a small parish gathering. Her relief in doing so was palpable. So, too, was the generosity and compassion shown by those who held her story with reverence. Over the years, I found that sharing my own story opened an avenue for others to do the same. Or that hearing another person's experience of grief provided healing in my own. Heart meets heart in such moments.

Unfortunately, there are too many instances where such sharing is not possible or even welcome. The effects of avoidance or denial of deep loss take a huge toll. In Mary's case, her husband's refusal to acknowledge his daughter's death resulted in severe dysfunction among their other four children. It was no wonder that some struggled with addiction and broken relationships later in life. While various factors were no doubt in play, unresolved grief affected the entire family system. This can happen even when a tragedy or loss remains buried. In some cases, it falls to others to piece together the pain that underlies such grief.

Author Fran Moskowitz was ten years old when she first learned that she had an older sister who had died at the age of five. It was a stunning revelation and a way of coming to understand her mother's deep sadness. "What puzzled me most was the depth of sorrow engendered by such a slim life span. I felt my mother's anguish was inexplicable, couldn't fathom why every visible trace of the child had been removed as though the clotting of pain was so fragile, that the merest shudder could see it to bleeding again" (*A Leak in the Heart*). After her mother's death, Moskowitz's father married a Holocaust survivor who had lost two sons in the death camps. One day, Moskowitz heard her stepmother yell at her six-year-old brother, "Why do you live when my sons are in the ground?" It was only in retrospect that Moskowitz could understand that the words were not directed at her brother but arose from her stepmother's deep pain. "How could we all have so misread her anguish? As if children were interchangeable and one could take the place of another."

SOCIETAL AVOIDANCE

Contemporary society's general discomfort with death doesn't help these situations. There seems to be an unwritten expectation that the window for grieving snaps shut after a month or two. After that, the bereaved person is encouraged to join a support group and then find "closure." As noted in my introduction, most of our resources on grief tend to cover the first year or two of one's bereavement and the initial stages of loss. Support systems and grief resources are incredibly helpful, to be sure, but they also have their limits. One frequent antidote offered to the bereaved is the recommendation to "stay busy."

In other words, don't dwell on it. Author Nancy Mairs countered such advice after the death of her husband. "Keep yourself busy, people say…The rationale behind [this]—that comfort and cheer depend on distraction, not contemplation, that only by denying some elements of one's life can one render that life supportable—repels me. And it leads, oddly, to more self-pity than I care to feel…An alternative response is to go all out with whatever you get handed, thinking about it like mad." She is quick to note that this doesn't mean dwelling on it or sinking into abject misery. Rather, it is vital to recognize that what we deny knowing can do greater harm in the end. "We are all going to die. And it is all right" (*Ordinary Time: Cycles in Marriage, Faith, and Renewal*).

Coupled with the denial of death is our collective tendency to avoid talking to others about their pain. Not knowing what to say, we say nothing. This only exacerbates the loneliness folded into the grieving process. It may start with neglecting to ask how the grieving person is doing or even to mention the deceased's name. Over time, anniversaries and birthdays pass without any acknowledgment or ability to share with anyone. In his book *A Grief Observed*, C.S. Lewis recorded the raw emotions that ensued after the death of his wife, Joy. To some, he appeared as an embarrassment and a reminder that they, too, would experience deep loss one day. "Perhaps," he wrote, "the bereaved ought to be isolated in special settlements like lepers."

At the same time, Lewis resisted talking about his wife and so avoided the subject himself. It took many years to recognize how I also avoided dealing with Jenny's death by overspiritualizing it. While Lewis initially directed much of his pain and anger at God, I withdrew into a vision of Jenny in an afterlife that sidestepped distressing questions about my faith or the reality of death. I rejected platitudes from others but devised ones of my own. This made me heroic to others at the time of her funeral and immediately afterward but, in the end, only magnified my loneliness and isolation. It also spared others the discomfort of trying to console me. We all have ways of coping with pain, and so I can look back at this time with a gentler gaze. Jenny's words of forgiveness in my dream were, in retrospect, an invitation to forgive myself. Once again, I found the grace to do so in the gift of stories and the generosity of others.

For Reflection *or* Conversation

How have you been affected by unacknowledged or disenfranchised grief?

What words of consolation have either helped or hindered your experience of grief?

What coping mechanisms did you develop in the immediate aftermath of your loss?

HEART TO HEART

To have been through something makes it easy to talk. One earns the right to understand—and give sympathy. We talk and talk and understand.

ANNE MORROW LINDBERGH

(*Hour of Gold, Hour of Lead*)

For several decades, I worked as a catechetical consultant. In this capacity, I I gave presentations, retreats, and days of reflection for catechists, pastoral ministers, parents, and women's organizations. Because these focused on spirituality and faith, they often included topics around grief and loss, healing, mercy, and forgiveness. To make a real-life connection, I would sometimes talk about Jenny's life and death. For the first few years, it was a painful process. Not only was it emotionally draining, but it also left me feeling as if I was losing touch with her by giving my story away. Over the years, however, it offered a sacred opening for others to share their own stories. Each time, I felt privileged to be entrusted with something so sacred.

This was the case several years ago when I directed a retreat for Native American women in New Mexico. After a lengthy drive to a remote retreat center, I arrived with a sense of uncertainty about what, if anything, I could offer them. The cultural divide seemed way too wide for me to cross. A small group gathered, and we chatted until the last attendee arrived. She was obviously distracted and upset, so we listened as she described her anxiety over her son's self-destructive behavior.

The other women were quick to offer support and consolation. From there, the retreat took a deeper turn as we shared mutual concerns over our children's lives. During our conversation, I spoke about Jenny. This provided an entrée into stories about the deaths of loved ones, sometimes in violent and traumatic ways. Empathy and compassion flowed, binding us together in both our suffering and our hope. While our worlds seemed miles apart, one woman's story gave way to the heart-to-heart encounters that transcend age, racial, religious, political, or cultural backgrounds, and life experiences.

In recounting the devastation that followed the death of her fourteen-year-old daughter—also named Jenny—Mirabai Starr describes the importance of simply showing up for her grief. "From the very beginning I suspected that something holy was happening and that if I were to push it away, I would regret it for the rest of my life. There was this sense of urgency, as if turning from death meant turning from my child. I wanted to offer Jenny the gift of my commitment to accompany her on her journey away from me, even if to do so simply meant dedicating my heartbeat and my breath to her and paying attention" (quoted in "Good Grief," Center for Action and Contemplation Daily Reflection, August 4, 2021).

Each time I encounter someone who is generous enough to share their own experience of loss, I feel enormously blessed. I also come to a greater understanding of the importance of remaining attuned to the very process of grief as it unfolds over time. While others may not acknowledge our losses, it is also easy to gloss over them ourselves. The costs of doing so are far too great. Disenfranchised grief can turn inward and generate mental, emotional, even physical harm. There is also a risk of losing something precious. Father Richard Rohr describes this as liminal space and a time of transformation. "We have to learn to remain open to our grief, to wait in patient expectation for what it has to teach us. When we close in too tightly around our sadness or our grief, when we try to fix it, control it, or understand it, we only deny ourselves its lessons" (*Beloved Sons Series: Men and Grief*). Such avoidance and denial seem to affect men more severely than women. Despite advances in avoiding gender-specific emotions, men are still under pressure to disguise or bluff their way through their feelings. I once heard this described succinctly: "Women congregate while men isolate." It holds true when it comes to dealing with grief and loss. While no one can fix us or take away the pain, the warmth of another's presence provides some respite and welcome relief from the ongoing pain of loss.

THE COMFORT OF COMPANIONSHIP

After great pain a formal feeling comes—
The Nerves sit ceremonious like Tombs—…
This is the Hour of Lead—
Remembered, if outlived,
As Freezing persons, recollect the Snow—
First—Chill—then Stupor—
then the letting go.

EMILY DICKINSON

The bereavement experience provides a different insight into the account of Thomas. Jesus enters the room and immediately extends a greeting of peace to a dazed and confused group of disciples. Then, knowing of Thomas' reticence to accept this phenomenal event of Resurrection, Jesus offers his own wounds as a place of refuge.

Such images have been common among Christian mystics who were drawn not to pretty images of a post-resurrected Jesus but to the sufferings of Christ's passion and death. Teresa of Avila experienced a radical turn toward contemplative prayer after encountering a statue depicting Jesus scourged and crowned with thorns. Julian of Norwich, after recovering from a life-threatening illness, drew closer to a vision of God's compassionate heart through her visions of Jesus. Rather than wallowing in such images, the hearts of each were opened further as compassion, mercy, and understanding took hold. Such is the enigmatic nature of suffering. In her book *Enduring Grace*,

Carol Lee Flinders notes how women mystics drew upon the suffering of Christ as a way of fervent meditation. This, in turn, gave them a sensitivity toward the workings of the human heart and the way in which suffering softens and opens it. "Having witnessed firsthand the simultaneity of joy and suffering with which a child enters the world—having seen the precious reward that can come of bloodshed and real agonies endured, they found paradoxical depths of meaning in the crucifixion that had eluded earlier Christian writers."

The intertwining of birth and death drew Anne Morrow Lindbergh through a torturous period in her life. In the aftermath of the kidnapping and murder of her eldest child, Charlie, she turned to her journal as an outlet for her bereavement and heartbreak. Much like that of C.S. Lewis, the journal moves through what we now identify as stages of grief. Lindbergh's was further complicated because, for two agonizing months, she didn't know if her son was alive or dead. When his body was discovered in a shallow grave a few miles from their home, the notorious nature of the crime and the fame of the Lindbergh name ramped up media coverage to an intolerable level. When she learned that she was once again pregnant, Lindbergh's joy was tinged with fear over what could be. She described feelings of insecurity and knowing the "nearness of death." The baby's birth, however, resulted in a radical embrace of new life:

> And I felt as if a great burden had fallen off me. I could not imagine the baby would do this for me, but I felt life given back to me—a door to life opened. I *wanted* to live, I felt the power to live. I was not afraid of death or life: a spell had been broken, the spell over us that made me

dread everything and feel that nothing would go right after this. The spell was broken by this real, tangible, perfect baby, coming into an imperfect world and coming out of the teeth of sorrow—a miracle. My faith had been reborn. (*Hour of Gold, Hour of Lead*)

Reading her words drew me back to that first year after Jenny's death and the news that I was once again pregnant. While I was exuberant over the prospect of another child, I feared that the baby would have the same intestinal disease that eventually took Jenny away from me. The memory of keeping vigil in a hospital over another ailing child was more than I could handle. After Eric was born—strong and healthy—I, too, knew what it was to savor a new life "coming out of the teeth of sorrow." Even so, it took decades to recognize the traumatizing effects of those anxious days by Jenny's bedside. Thus, my disturbing dreams about forgetting her or neglecting her care were often set against the backdrop of the hospital. After Eric was born, I struggled with the fear that he, too, would take sick and die. Ron provided a steady presence that kept me from becoming overprotective and manic about every sniffle or sneeze. I would also recall the strange and yet prescient comment from an acquaintance who, upon seeing Eric for the first time, said, "He's not Jenny II." Odd as it was, the observation reminded me that children are *not* interchangeable and that Eric would grow in his own way.

Lindbergh's decision to publish her diaries and thus share her private anguish over Charlie's death was based on the important need to connect with others. "To suffer is to be alone," she wrote. "To watch another suffer is to know the barrier that shuts each of us away by himself. Only individuals can suffer." In a sense, she allowed others—including me—to find a bit of refuge in her wounds and to recognize the grace that emerges when suffering is shared. Empathy expands through attuning ourselves to the pain of others. The "hour of lead" turns to gold as we let go of our chill and stupor in order to reach out and embrace others. No wonder those undergoing deep loss recognize, in hindsight, the grace in the wound. Doing so takes time and an attentiveness to our deepest needs.

FINDING REFUGE

In seeking such attentiveness, we also become aware of reaching the opposite extreme. The counterpoint to encounters with others is the danger of overextending ourselves as we seek out those who have suffered similar losses. It is all too easy to move from being *part* of a support group to *becoming* that support for others. Flora Slosson Wuellner describes how, after the death of her husband, she was drawn into serving others without regard for her own well-being. In an article on wounded healers, she describes how loving service without healthy boundaries led to physical and spiritual depletion. While trying to internalize another's grief, she found her own increasing. "There is an incredible difference between an interaction in which power goes *out* of us, and an encounter in which power goes *forth* from us. The first implies depletion, and the second a renewed flowing forth of strength" ("'Reach Out Your Hand, and Put It in My Side,'" *Weavings*, Vol. VIII, no. 5). This marks the difference between an infected wound and one that is in the process of healing.

This can happen when we jump very quickly into trying to support others without placing healthy boundaries around ourselves. In some cases, it is a handy way to shut down the arduous process of bereavement. More often, however, it may be an attempt to seek a way through the morass of pain, loneliness, and unanswered questions.

This was brought home to me shortly after Jenny's funeral. As a mother of two children with physical and developmental challenges, Madelyn (not her real name) became a fierce advocate for those with special needs. When Ron and I first arrived in Sitka, she met us with open arms and offered tremendous support as we sought information about Down syndrome and the best way to help Jenny thrive, both mentally and physically. Madelyn was instrumental in establishing programs and pushing for legislation that made Alaska a forerunner in the understanding of and care for those with disabilities. Her tireless efforts paved the way for a new understanding and acceptance of those with physical and developmental challenges, both in our community and throughout the state. Even so, there was a limit to what she could do.

After our return from Denver, where Jenny's funeral and burial took place, Madelyn came to visit me. As she began to talk, it seemed like she was addressing herself more than me. She began to recount her experiences and said that, after her own children's diagnoses were revealed, she was fine. She named the challenges she faced as various aspects of their physical and developmental needs were uncovered. "I was in control," she repeated after each one. Then she paused and began to cry. "But now Jenny is dead, and I am not in control anymore." I have often wondered if this was the moment—

finally—that Madelyn was able to find a place of refuge. While her service to and on behalf of others was vital and truly admirable, it also kept her from acknowledging her own limitations. Grief has a way of bringing us to our knees in humble recognition that we are not in control of our own lives, let alone the lives of others. In reflecting on the account of Thomas and his encounter with the risen Christ, Wuellner notes the tenderness of touch and the place of refuge in the story. "The wounds are not only to be seen, but to be touched and entered. There is an intimate power, a connectedness present as we with Thomas are invited to put our hands within the wound of Jesus, which leads to the heart of God." To do so is to acknowledge our limitations and our need for boundaries, for humility, and for attentiveness to self-care. Heart-to-heart encounters—when they aren't attempts to fix one another but simply to remain present to each other's pain—play a large role in providing balance.

Our return to Sitka after the funeral offered a few days of respite before Ron reported for duty at the Coast Guard base. Given the small size of the town and the restrictions of its island locale, we headed to the top of a nearby mountain. A large cloud bank hovered over the city, but we remained high above it. After several months of near-constant gray and gloomy weather, the sunlight was a balm to heart and soul. I was well aware of the need to descend the mountain and re-enter the dark expanse of grief. For just a moment, however, I found a place to rest, to be still, and to allow myself to be held by the warmth of the sun and the love I shared with Ron. Looking back, I can see how we followed our instincts in just the right way. Much as we appreciated the outpouring of sympathy from friends and coworkers, we needed a place of refuge.

The tender touch that Jesus extends to Thomas is a reminder of this need. Over the years, I have answered similar calls to find places in the sun. One loss doesn't make others that follow any easier or less painful. Each one, however, teaches us to go easy on ourselves and to embrace the moments and places of refuge where our wounded hearts have a chance to pulse with life, ever so slightly, once again.

For Reflection *or* Conversation

Where have you found refuge during a time of grief and loss?

What has helped you let go of fear, anxiety, dread, or anger in order to open yourself to new life?

How have you been a place of refuge for others during times of grief?

Three
From Transmittal to Transformation
Unresolved Grief

When they had finished breakfast, Jesus said to Simon Peter, "Simon, son of John, do you love me more than these?" He said to him, "Yes, Lord, you know that I love you." He said to him, "Feed my lambs." He then said to him a second time, "Simon, son of John, do you love me?" He said to him, "Yes, Lord, you know that I love you." He said to him, "Tend my sheep."

He said to him the third time, "Simon, son of John, do you love me?" Peter was distressed that he had said to him a third time, "Do you love me?" and he said to him, "Lord, you know everything; you know that I love you." [Jesus] said to him, "Feed my sheep." "Amen, amen, I say

> *to you, Amen, amen, I say to you, when you were younger, you used to dress yourself and go where you wanted; but when you grow old, you will stretch out your hands, and someone else will dress you and lead you where you do not want to go."* *He said this signifying by what kind of death he would glorify God. And when he had said this, he said to him, "Follow me."* JOHN 21:15-19

There are several instances in the Gospels where Jesus poses a question and then provides no answers that bring his teachings to a tidy end. The post-Resurrection exchange with Peter is a case in point. The questions are puzzling and even hurtful to Peter, and yet they serve as an act of mercy. After denying his relationship with Jesus three times, he is offered three chances to state his love and devotion. It lets him off the hook and gives him an out from guilt and regret.

Others aren't so lucky. Unresolved grief often results in endless cycles of blame directed at oneself and others. It may also be accompanied by unrelenting regret. This, in turn, leads to a morass of depression, guilt, and feelings of worthlessness. Richard Rohr names this succinctly: "What we don't transform, we transmit." The heart shattered by loss has the potential to wound others when we don't know how or where to take the pain. This comes as no surprise to anyone involved with therapy or spiritual direction. Anger—one of the common and initial stages of grief—becomes sustained and may be directed at others in a show of resentment or blame. Anger drawn inward can result in severe and sustained depression. Like a terrible vortex fueled by rage, guilt, loneliness, and fear, it drags us down and may require therapy, medication, and lots of inner work to emerge from it. The cultural messages to "move on" or get over it are far from adequate for someone in this state. And the more it continues, the harder it becomes to transform it into something life-giving and hopeful. Author and educator Parker Palmer describes this as being "hollowed out by loss." In his blog, he noted, "Maybe the most common obstacle to holding our losses well—apart from physical or mental pain—is a failure of imagination about ways to redeem them" (Facebook post, October 1, 2021).

This is not to point fingers or place blame on those wounded by loss. Quite the contrary. Palmer knows first-hand the suffering caused by deep depression. He describes his own experience of clinical depression with sensitivity toward what it entails and what it takes to deal with it. Thus, the "failure of imagination" may well come from a culture that is unwilling to accept death for what it is or to offer the tender touch and gentle presence that a grieving person needs over the long term.

I was fortunate in my own experience to be married to someone who didn't find the need to close off or deny the pain we both felt after Jenny's death. Unlike Mary, the woman whose husband wouldn't discuss their daughter's death, I was able to talk to Ron—and he with me—about the pain of our loss. Jenny remained a vital part of our lives, albeit in a different form.

I was also offered solace from a compassionate and understanding minister, Father James Miller. He was newly assigned to our parish as pastor; we met him for the first time after returning to Sitka after Jenny's funeral. Over the next several months, he became a source of consolation as he gently drew me into involvement at the church while remaining ever aware of the loss we had suffered. Rather than serving as a distraction from Jenny's death, the activity became a way for me to re-engage with the community and find strength to carry on each day. This led to an appreciation of the "feeding" aspect of Jesus' injunction to Peter and what it means to minister to others. It is a delicate process that involves piecing one's life back together even while recognizing that it will never be the same. Those involved in ministering to the bereaved recognize the importance of striking a balance between helping them attend to their loss while also offering hope and trust in God and in the future.

I found an apt analogy for this delicate process after visiting Winchester Cathedral—the magnificent medieval structure in Hampshire, England—and learning the story behind its clerestory window. In the seventeenth century, a group of soldiers, celebrating after a recent victory in battle, overran the cathedral and, in a drunken spree, smashed its magnificent stained glass windows. After the soldiers' departure, the heartbroken residents of Winchester retrieved the bits of glass and placed them in storage for eighteen years. Putting them back together in the original pattern proved impossible, so the shards were used to create a striking mosaic for the huge west window that illuminates the cathedral to this day.

Any degree of loss can leave us with shattered hearts. Moving through a process of grieving entails picking up the shards and piecing them back together again. Although the heart will never have the same shape and contours as before, it can remain open to the light. In this way, grief offers the possibility of transformation—a process that usually transpires as a result of great awe or great suffering. Transformation is essential to the spiritual journey. "Without it, we remain anxious, mean-spirited, narrow-minded, intolerant, self-absorbed, caught up in petty pursuits, shackled by our addictions, a burden to ourselves, hurtful toward others and the earth. We leave the world a worse place than we found it" (Thomas Hart, *Spiritual Quest: A Guide to the Spiritual Landscape*). This explains why the great mystics placed a value on suffering. It was not in pursuit of masochistic or overly ascetic self-martyrdom. Rather, they recognized its transformative power to open themselves to love and to be loved more generously.

Another striking aspect of the story of the cathedral window is how the residents of Winchester stored the pieces for so many years. Our contemporary attitude toward grief would not countenance such a long period of waiting. While we are quick to assure the grieving that "time heals all wounds," we set parameters for just how much time is allowed before moving on. We are in such a rush to promote the idea of healing that we miss the understanding of grief's extended realities. This was the case after the 1999 shooting at Columbine High School. At the time, I was working as a pastoral minister in Littleton, Colorado. While students in our parish mostly attended another school, they and their parents were deeply affected by the tragedy. Even as students fled the school on live television, commentators were questioning when healing for the community might begin. It was a stunning denial of the devastation that could not be wrapped up neatly in a matter of days, weeks, or months. All these years later, the wound cuts deep in the community and in those who continue to grieve the deaths of their children and friends as well as those who witnessed and survived the trauma of peers gunning down their classmates.

More recently, a brutal event in Uvalde, Texas, took the lives of nineteen fourth graders and two of their teachers. As with other school shootings, the press turned to survivors of the Columbine tragedy for their recollections as well as their counsel for those in shock and mourning. Now that they have children of their own, many of these survivors have a perspective that can only come from years of processing their pain and piecing their lives back together. In doing so, they provide consolation that touches others in a heartfelt and realistic manner. President Joe Biden, who experienced the deaths of two of his children, empathized with the families in a way that only someone who knows such loss could do. In the wake of the Uvalde tragedy, he said, "To lose a child is like having a piece of your soul ripped away. There's a hollowness in your chest and you feel like you're being sucked into it and never going to be able to get out. It's suffocating. And it's never quite the same" (May 24, 2022, Address to the Nation). A shattered heart takes time to be pieced together again. In the interim we, like those long-ago residents of Winchester, must simply hold the fragments and trust in the long and slow process of re-formation.

For Reflection *or* Conversation

When have you been "hollowed out by loss"?

What does it take to piece a broken heart back together?

How have you held your grief in a sacred space over the long term?

From Transmittal to Transformation

LAYERS OF LOSS

Whether a loss is personal or communal, it takes time to uncover the layers that underlie the initial experience. To this day, I cannot see a child with Down syndrome and not think of Jenny and all that we missed in not seeing her grow past her first birthday. Because most of her life was spent far away from our extended families, few of those family members have any memory of her. This exacerbates the loneliness that comes each year with the marking of her birthday and the anniversary of her death. Her siblings were born after she died, so what they know of her comes through photographs and the sharing of our memories. I could not have foreseen any of this in the immediate wake of her death.

Since that time, I have experienced other significant losses—the deaths of both of my parents and all three of my sisters, one of whom died the morning of another sister's funeral. Each death uncovered additional layers of loss that took months, even years, to emerge. My mother reveled in hosting holiday parties and family events. When my father died, she was no longer able to live alone. One loss followed another when she sold her house and, with it, the hosting capabilities that drew our large family together. In time, my sister Corinne began to assume the role of convener. Her home became the locus for holiday meals and other festivities. With her passing and the subsequent sale of her house by her daughters, the center of our family life seemed to dissipate. It's a loss we are still unpacking.

This is another aspect of bereavement that receives little attention, particularly as the years pass. Within a family, the dynamics shift after one member is no longer present. The recognition of systemic change in a faith or civic community can go unacknowledged and unresolved for decades. In addition, the experience of multiple deaths in a short span of time—much like my three sisters dying so close together—makes it even harder to process each one.

In some cases, we remain frozen in the process of bereavement and unable to move forward. This might lead to making the loss a permanent part of one's identity. I recognized this as a potential danger during the viewing of baby pictures with my family. As I wrote in chapter 1, my two children laughing at the sight of Jenny's photo jarred me into realizing that I needn't spend the rest of my life being the bereaved mother. Not only would this have stymied my own well-being, but it would also have impacted my family. I have distant relatives whose daughter died at the age of six after suffering respiratory failure. The first thing you saw when entering their home was a huge portrait of their daughter in the living room. I could only imagine how this affected their two other children, both of whom were adopted after the daughter's death. The mother's inability to let go made the enshrinement of her daughter's memory a looming presence in the household. As the surviving children grew into adulthood, one developed anorexia and died at a young age. The other became estranged from her mother and cut off all ties after her father's death. I can't speak to what else transpired in the home, but the mother's fixed identity as perpetually mourning her dead child could not have helped.

The opposite end of the spectrum is that of an identity wrapped around one's self-image as stoic, strong, and proud of one's ability to withstand pain. Parker Palmer calls this "living at high altitude" and notes the crash landing that occurs when all these illusions fall away. Death has a way of grounding us. The way I overspiritualized Jenny's death by telling myself and others that she was at peace, that I completely trusted in God's love and mercy despite the dark dreams and solitary times of sadness, was one way of staying above the clouds. Palmer notes that his own was a result of other factors: training as an intellectual and dwelling more in his head than his heart; embracing an abstract notion of God rather than pursuing a relationship with God; and masking his true self out of fear of dissembling his public persona. Burying one's grief under a layer of falsehood only leads to greater heartache and pain. What we deny knowing does enormous damage.

FORGIVING TO FORGET

Another layer of loss has to do with the need for mercy. Some years ago, I was invited to give a presentation at an Elderhostel on the topic of forgiveness. Much like my experience with Native American women in New Mexico, I felt intimidated by the perceived gap with those I would be addressing. As a woman in her mid-thirties, what sort of insights could I offer to those in their seventies and eighties? I began by showing a film clip of an ongoing rift between an older woman and her adult daughter. The scene triggered a rich discussion about various forms of alienation and damaged relationships. Once again, it turned out differently than I imagined. I was there less as an expert on the topic of forgiveness and more as a facilitator around its transformative power. At the end of the gathering, one woman, a Benedictine sister, raised a question that stymied me: How do you forgive someone who is dead? She went on to describe her father's abuse toward her mother and the difficulty she had in releasing her anger and resentment.

The author and humorist David Sedaris describes a similar situation in his book *Happy-Go-Lucky*. In a May 31, 2022, *Fresh Air* interview with host Terry Gross, he detailed his fraught relationship with his father. Unlike the title of his latest book, the process of releasing his hurt and resentment was far from happy. Despite his father's mellowed countenance at the end of his life, Sedaris noted the difficulty of forgiving the decades-long abuse and cruelty he suffered at his father's hands. Even so, he noted the important need of "laying down the gauntlet" so he could move forward.

Both scenarios reveal a harsh truth around the complex nature of grief. How to forgive someone when reconciliation is no longer possible? When does the weight of resentment become corrosive to one's emotional well-being? Is it feasible—or even advisable—to forget? What does it mean to forgive both the living and the dead?

I didn't have ready answers for the question during the Elderhostel presentation, but now, through the benefit of hindsight and personal experience, I recognize the vital nature of such forgiveness. Rather than excusing or rationalizing another person's bad behavior, forgiveness offers an out from self-destructive cycles of anger, resentment, fear, and other toxic emotions. This in turn minimizes the possibility of transmitting one's pain by directing it at others or turning it inward. Forgiveness relinquishes the power that another person or experience might have over us. This makes the words of Jesus to Peter an invitation as well as an extension of forgiveness.

From Transmittal to Transformation

Bud Welch discovered this in a profound way when his only child, Julie Marie, was killed in the 1994 bombing of the Murrah Federal Building in Oklahoma City. Welch initially reacted to his daughter's death with rage directed at the perpetrators of the violence. He drank to excess and dreamed of violent retribution. About a year after her death, Welch recognized the need to move forward rather than wallowing in his anger and pain. After seeing a picture of Bill McVeigh—the father of one of the bombers—bent over in anguish, he recognized their shared experience of grief. He reached out, and the two men became friends. Across this great divide, Welch started to acknowledge and embrace the need for forgiveness. In a post on John Noltner's blog *A Peace of My Mind*, Welch noted the benefit of mercy: "Forgiveness doesn't do a damn thing for the killers. You totally release yourself. That's where the good comes from."

What gets forgotten in such an experience is not the extent of damage done to us but the need to retain its power to continue doing so. When we reach this point, we find that our only regret is holding onto the past. The more we forgive, the more we can forget the importance of clinging to resentment and anger. In leaving the past behind, we have the freedom to move forward and to acquire a deeper will to live and to love.

PERSPECTIVE AND CONTEXT

Fourteen years after Jenny's death, Ron and I wrote a book about our individual experiences. We chose to do so through letters from each of us that were addressed to her, along with select entries from my journal that were written during my pregnancy and up until the days following her death. Even though we had talked through the experience with one another, reading each other's letters was revelatory. It provided an understanding of how each of us dealt with and processed her birth, her multiple surgeries and hospitalizations, the blessed months in which she thrived, and then her death. While I made a few unsuccessful attempts at getting it published, the book was clearly written for the two of us and out of a need to unravel some of the complexities of our individual and joint experiences. Such a project would not have been as honest or as insightful had it been written in the first year or so of our bereavement. It took time to reach an understanding of the impact it had on each of us. Over thirty years have passed, and yet I continue to uncover new insights within this collection of letters. This is why I lean toward the word "grace" when considering the long-term experience of grief. Those haunting years in the wake of Jenny's death mellowed over the decades into a deep gratitude for life and an opening to mystery—particularly the mysterious grace of God. Time lends perspective.

It also allows for contextual insight. If can be easy to approach bereavement in monolithic fashion, as if the rest of our lives is put on hold while we mourn our loss. Ron and I were both in our mid- to late twenties during that period. We underwent other massive changes due to our recent marriage

From Transmittal to Transformation

and moves across the country (twice in one year). This gave rise to questions about where each of us wanted to settle and what direction our lives would take. Ron wrote honestly about this in one of his letters: "As has always been the case in my life, much of my focus and energy was directed within, that is trying to figure out what my life was about. Because of this I become oblivious, at times, to what is going on outside of me...I often need to be dragged out of myself by the events going on around me." His words recall the "first half of life" issues we were each dealing with—ones that had to do with our joint and individual paths. He knew the Coast Guard was not going to stretch into a career, and I had given up teaching elementary school while questioning how I might pursue my interest in ministry and spiritual direction.

It is also striking to recall another significant death that we didn't have a chance to process. Ron's father died just weeks after we settled in Sitka and, given the rapid changes happening with Jenny and our new home, Ron had little time to absorb the loss, let alone move through the grieving process. Thus did the pain of one loss become compounded by another.

Several years ago, I attended the burial of a coworker's mother. I drove to and from the cemetery with two friends. As is often the case with funerals, we began telling stories about deaths that continued to affect each of us. We all knew the importance of sharing such experiences and then lamented how we had little time to do so; we all had to get back to work. After my miscarriage, I recalled a story about my grandmother, who was devastated after having a second miscarriage. Her sisters, worried about her state of mind, wouldn't allow her to walk by herself at a nearby park for fear she would throw herself into the lake. "Poor Nanny," I thought. "She had no grief resources to help her through those times." As if she were by my side, I heard her respond, "Poor Kathy. She has no time to grieve."

While so many bereavement processes focus on the first or second year after the death of a loved one, it can be hard to find the time for them. Those whose spouses have died describe how much of their energy is taken up with sorting out finances, filling in forms, dealing with legalities, and clearing out possessions and property. The emotional toll is exacerbated by physical and mental exhaustion in having to deal with so many details.

For these reasons, it is even more important to give oneself an expanse of time in which to recognize and acknowledge the larger picture of one's experience. As I reread the letters I wrote to Jenny fourteen years ago, I see even more clearly how I over-spiritualized the experience. It was my way of coping with the pain, the fear and risk of having another child, and the long road of grief that lay ahead of me. Gaining perspective allows us to recall the path of grief and how we traversed it.

THE DARK NIGHT

Even though I walk through the valley of the shadow of death, I will fear no evil, for you are with me; your rod and your staff comfort me.
PSALM 23:4

In observing his own bereavement after the death of his wife, C.S. Lewis described grief as a valley. This image resonates with Psalm 23, a common reading for funerals. Even though the rest of the psalm is lighter in tone and texture, the line about the "valley of the shadow of death" speaks strongly to those encountering a devastating loss. Echoing the sentiments expressed by President Biden at the time of the Uvalde tragedy, Lewis pondered the lasting effect on a parent whose child has died and how it is one of those losses that is never "gotten over." "Never in any place or time, will she have her son on her knees, or bathe him, or tell him a story or plan for his future, or see her grandchild" (*A Grief Observed*).

Despite the heavy image of a traversing a dark valley, Lewis also noted that it was not a circular path. Such is the difference between a depression which hopes for life to return to the way it was and the "dark night" in which one accepts the permanent nature of the loss. This is the nature of transformation, which has the potential to take us to a new place. In an essay on wounded healers, Deborah Smith-Douglas describes how Lewis came to recognize and resolve the long-term effects of his wife's death. "For Lewis, the transforming insight in his own grief and loneliness was not a glib assurance that he would get over his shattering loss, but that God had not left him alone in his sorrow. Presence, not 'recovery' was what enabled him to believe again that 'all shall be well'" ("Wounded and Healed," *Weavings*, Vol. XV, no. 2). This is certainly not the kind of "closure" so often associated with the grieving process, but it is a reality for those who cross the dark valley and come to place of acceptance. As Smith-Douglas notes, these losses, while intolerable in terms of their lifelong impact, can also provide the courage, trust, and generosity of spirit needed "to live close to the heart of God and to live toward the promised day of resurrection, whose joy no eye has seen nor human heart imagined (1 Cor 2:9)."

The invitation that Jesus extends to Peter implies this kind of transformation. By letting go of remorse, guilt, and other entrapments, Peter is free to follow Jesus in a new way. For all of us, there are places we would rather not go. The death of loved ones and other forms of loss is one of them. Even so, the freedom to move on, to piece one's life together in a new mosaic of love and acceptance, to feed others as well as oneself, and to transform the pain into something grace-filled leads to a welcome mellowness of heart that comes only with time, patience, and an openness to what can be.

For Reflection *or* Conversation

What other forms of unresolved grief can you name?

What helped you to transform your pain rather than transmit it?

How have you known the freedom that comes with forgiveness and mercy?

Four
Mellowness of Heart

The Long View

As they approached the village to which they were going, he gave the impression that he was going on farther. But they urged him, "Stay with us, for it is nearly evening and the day is almost over." So he went in to stay with them. And it happened that, while he was with them at table, he took bread, said the blessing, broke it, and gave it to them. With that their eyes were opened and they recognized him, but he vanished from their sight. Then they said to each other, "Were not our hearts burning [within us] while he spoke to us on the way and opened the scriptures to us?" So they set out at once and returned to Jerusalem where they found gathered together the eleven and

> *those with them who were saying, "The Lord has truly been raised and has appeared to Simon!" Then the two recounted what had taken place on the way and how he was made known to them in the breaking of the bread.* LUKE 24:28-35

In her introduction to Lewis' book *A Grief Observed*, Madeleine L'Engle shared the experience of her husband's death and what followed it. "Perhaps I have never felt more closely the strength of God's presence than I did during the months of my husband's dying and after his death." Even though the devastation was severe—she describes it as an "amputation"—there was consolation as well.

I experienced something similar prior to and in the wake of Jenny's death. Her last days were an agonizing succession of daily trips to the doctor where I pleaded for help as I watched her slipping away from us. At the time, we were living in an apartment on the edge of Sitka's shoreline. A week or so before her death, after placing Jenny in Ron's arms, I went outside, where I watched the water crashing against the rocks. I felt my own heart battered with the same ferocity by waves of uncertainty, fear, anxiety, and anger. As Jenny continued to lose weight and grow more listless each day, I railed at God for not doing something to help. After venting for a lengthy period, something shifted. I felt God's tears intermingled with my own. It startled me but also came as a revelation. I began to see the entire situation not as the willful doing of an impersonal and distant entity, but one of being held by a Divine force who longed as much as I did for Jenny's health and well-being. This same sense remained as an undercurrent to the tumult that assailed me in the days and months to follow. Over the span of decades it has increased, paradoxically through additional experiences of loss.

The death of a loved one—particularly one's child—results in a hole in the heart that will never be healed. It can, however, be filled with something different: the mysterious grace of God. This entails a re-forming of the heart, a process that unfolds and cannot be forced, rushed, or planned. Its subtlety can also take us by surprise—much like the unsuspecting disciples who encounter a redemptive presence amid their sorrow. The eyes of the Emmaus disciples open to the presence of Christ: not through hours of conversation and scriptural explorations but in the simple act of breaking bread together. What follows is a "burning of the heart" which propels them out of their individual grief and into a new recognition of Divine presence. No wonder this account has been applied to various experiences of conversion and a radical altering of the heart. Opening with a scene of grieving disciples, it reveals how the brokenhearted can find their way toward something better than "closure": a path to a new and more open-hearted life.

FORMING A NEW HEART

I will give you a new heart, and a new spirit I will put within you. I will remove the heart of stone from your flesh and give you a heart of flesh. EZEKIEL 36:26

Every major religious tradition has belief in the alchemy that can transform suffering into something greater. Christian belief in the Paschal Mystery embraces the hope that life emerges from death, that light breaks through the darkness. Resurrection differs from resuscitation, however. This helps to explain why the Emmaus couple, along with Mary, Thomas, and other disciples, had trouble recognizing Jesus during their encounters with him. In each one, an extension of tenderness opens their eyes and alters their perceptions. Folded into Peter's post-Resurrection account is the added dimension of forgiveness and liberation. In the invitation to confess his love for Jesus, Peter is also offered an out from his guilt and shame. This enables him to move forward and follow his spiritual path, even while taking him to places he would rather not go.

As a spiritual director, I am familiar with the way in which unacknowledged or unresolved grief adds to one's spiritual malaise and distress. It takes a great deal of inner work to uncover what lies at the center of our pain as well as the deep longing for grace. When grief remains buried, denied, hidden, or unrecognized, we become mired in the hurt, the anger, the loneliness, the utter hopelessness. This is when we are likely to transmit the pain rather than transform it. The hardened heart—something warned against in the Bible—becomes brittle, rigid, closed off, and lacking in compassion or empathy.

Transformative grief, on the other hand, offers a way toward the "heart of flesh"—one open to both heartfelt joy and heartbreaking sorrow. Robert A. Johnson describes this as "transformation into informed wholeness," something he experienced in dramatic fashion. At the age of eleven, Johnson was caught in a collision between two cars. The impact crushed his right knee, resulting in the amputation of his leg. Since he was positioned in such a way that one leg was on the sidewalk while the other was in the path of the collision, he could easily have lost both legs and even his life. As he lay in serious condition in the hospital, he drifted from death, due to massive blood loss, toward what he describes as a "Golden World." The experience colored the remainder of his life and contributed to his later work as a Jungian analyst. In his book *Balancing Heaven and Earth*, he notes how the experience "wounded me enough to ground me, but not so much as to knock all the life out of me." This is what becomes possible when we start to discover the grace within the wound. While there is no blueprint for such a process, some common factors make it possible. We find three possibilities folded into the Emmaus experience.

CLOSE ENCOUNTERS

One of the most striking aspects of the Emmaus account occurs after the disciples recognize Jesus in the breaking of the bread. Their first inclination is not to search for Jesus, who vanishes from their sight, but to return to their community and share their astounding revelation. In doing so, they don't seek a return to what was but move forward and in sync with others who understand the depth of their transformative experience. They also opt to be with those who could share not only their wonder at the new revelation of Christ in their midst but also the trauma of having witnessed a brutal execution.

Perhaps this why Luke, a physician, chose to place the account of the Emmaus journey within the context of community. The story opens with the two disciples discussing "all the things that had occurred" and "looking downcast." Rather than revealing himself immediately and thereby offering the disciples a respite from their pain, Jesus gives them time to talk it out and offers them, through his interpretation of the scriptures, a broader way to view their experience. This may have constituted part of the sharing they offered when gathering once again with their larger community.

So it is with those whose grief has mellowed over time. It gives them an increased capacity for empathy and an ability to talk about suffering and death without the discomfort that so often accompanies these topics. No wonder the most effective counselors and leaders of bereavement groups are those who have walked the way of loss and devastation. One of these is Anne Marie Mahoney, a bereavement group facilitator who generously shared her insights and expertise with me as part of the writing of this book. In one of our conversations, she pointed out the "rules" for a bereavement group that include things *not* to say, such as "I know just how you feel" or "Things will get better." Platitudes are unhelpful, no matter who offers them.

By contrast, those who allow a re-formation of the heart understand the value of silent companionship. "The friend who can be silent with us in a moment of despair or confusion, who can stay with us in an hour of grief and bereavement, who can tolerate not knowing, not curing, not healing, and face with us the reality of our powerlessness, that is a friend who cares" (Henri Nouwen, *The Road to Daybreak: A Spiritual Journey*). Thus, we needn't worry about what should be said to a grieving person; rather, we should question how best to be present to that person.

Circumstances around a loss make each one unique and, as such, require a particular way to settle in one's heart and memory. As I noted in chapter 1, my recurring dreams about forgetting or neglecting Jenny lasted for several years. It took even longer to recognize that, in addition to her death, I was traumatized by her repeated hospitalizations. Trauma is another layer of grief that is easily overlooked and then forgotten in the immediate aftermath of a devastating loss. When we draw together through mutual support and understanding, recognition of these layers dawns and true healing can begin.

A key aspect of such support is the grace that comes through small acts of kindness. I recall many of these in the days and weeks after Jenny's death. Officials at the Coast Guard base in Sitka arranged for Jenny's body to be flown to Denver for her funeral and took care of the airline reservations for Ron and me. My sister-in-law Willie took care of the funeral arrangements and gathered my young nieces together to sing during the liturgy. As I entered the church, four-year-old Shannon approached and shyly handed me a handmade card—one which I cherish to this day. Upon our return to Sitka, we received extensions of outreach from our parish, the Coast Guard, and the special needs community. One of the most touching was a visit from a woman named Mary. When I opened the door, she simply held out her arms and took me into her warm embrace. She gave me a soft wool blanket that, along with the blanket made by our friend Liz, still provides warmth and comfort all these years later.

None of these memories involve eloquent words or grand gestures. Rather, like the simple act of breaking bread, they open the eyes and warm the heart. It echoes the gorgeous poem by Naomi Shihab Nye in which she writes about the intertwining of sorrow and kindness and how we must know the first before understanding the second (*The Words Under the Words*). At our most tender and vulnerable moments, kindness is a balm like no other.

MEMORY AND RECOGNITION

Another striking aspect of the Emmaus account is how the disciples spend most of the day with Jesus and yet still don't recognize him. They have inklings, however, as their hearts respond to his teaching. In the end, the memory and ritual of breaking bread results in full-blown realization.

As with many Down syndrome children, Jenny was slow in developing physical and verbal skills. She never learned to crawl and didn't roll over until after the colostomy was resectioned. For a few weeks after the surgery, she thrived as she felt more freedom of movement. It was a bit like watching a butterfly emerge from a chrysalis. Shortly after her birth, I was given two gifts that became even more meaningful after her death. One was a cloisonné butterfly necklace. The other was a copy of *Hope for the Flowers* by Trina Paulus—the transformative story of two caterpillars turning into butterflies. I drew upon each of these gifts as I pondered questions around Jenny's short life and what I envisioned as a life beyond one I could know or imagine. For years, I wore the necklace on her birthday and on the anniversary of her death. I chose yellow roses for her funeral because of the connection with *Hope for the Flowers*. To this day, I cannot see a yellow butterfly without sensing Jenny's closeness.

Such associations—through a song, a poem, or an aspect of nature—are not unusual for those who mourn the loss of a loved one. In her work as a bereavement group facilitator, Anne Marie Mahoney describes the helpful use of music, poetry, film, and other creative means to generate associations and rekindle memories. They are valuable connecting points that, over time, lose the sense of sadness from their original association and mellow into something warm and consoling.

There is also power in ritual. It is not surprising that religions and cultures around the world and throughout the ages developed powerful ways to mourn the dead through elaborate ceremonies. From the Irish wake to the Jewish shiva, from Hindu funeral pyres to New Orleans jazz processions, the human need for ritualizing death is apparent. Even when no formal ritual takes place, the spontaneous erection of floral shrines and the staging of candlelight vigils at sites of mass shootings and other tragic events speak to a collective need to make sense of the pain as well as to draw together in mutual support.

MOVING FORWARD

As noted earlier, the Emmaus disciples don't spend time searching for Jesus or trying to reclaim their earlier experiences. They rush back to tell their fellow disciples about their encounter and the revelation of Christ in their midst. As with the other post-Resurrection encounters, the disciples recognize a new reality and move forward to meet it.

There comes a point in the grieving process in which we get through a day without remembering the one who has died. This might lead, at first, to guilt and remorse as we question whether we have been remiss in failing to remember someone so close to our hearts. When grief moves along a healthy path, however, we come to view this as another step along the way rather than a deficiency in ourselves. It's part of the realization mentioned in chapter 2 and the untangling of grief from our identity. Constance Fitzgerald, a Carmelite sister, described this as part of a "purification" in which memory loses its power to define our entire personhood. Sorrow has a particular way of opening the heart and enabling us to love more deeply.

Such grief can be experienced in a very personal way or in one that encompasses mass injustice and extensive tragedy. Arn Chorn witnessed the murder of his parents during the slaughter perpetrated by the Khmer Rouge in Cambodia. It haunted him for decades and left him feeling impotent in trying to find his way toward love and justice. His traumatic memories started to morph into something else as he learned about victims of other tragedies. "I began to realize that there are many victims. Finally…I have come to realize that I am alive again. I can love and trust again. I can feel the suffering of others, not just my own. I can suffer not just for the Cambodians, but for the millions more who suffer today" (quoted in Luther E. Smith, Jr., "Earth Has No Sorrow that Heaven Cannot Heal," *Weavings*, Vol. VIII, no. 5).

There is a great paradox in such an experience—one that finds a way forward through empathy and the ability to share one's pain with others. Melissa Kelley describes how grief can form a bond with others who know the devastation of loss and the lonely road of bereavement. "Loss changes us," she writes. "There is no returning to what life was like before the loss." While others may sympathize, the ones who know first-hand what such an experience entails can become our greatest help in navigating this new territory. This helps to explain why so many marriages break up in the wake of a child's death. If one person moves forward while the other remains stuck, the possibility of staying in sync diminishes.

Grief support groups serve as important settings for sharing our experiences and finding an understanding of this long and painful process. In her booklet *Helping Teens with Grief* (Twenty-Third Publications), Margaret Felice offers sage advice to young people about the value of support groups. "Nearly everyone I know who has participated in support groups went in skeptical and came out feeling supported. Spending a few hours with people going through similar experiences can make apparent a truth you may need reminding of through this process: You are not alone."

That last line may be the most important aspect of moving through the grieving process. When the sadness abates, recognition of the bond we share with others begins to arise. Like Arn Chorn, we find a sense of solidarity with others who have suffered a similar loss—parents and grandparents of children who have died, widows and widowers, victims of violent acts and relatives of those who perpetrate them, survivors of great tragedies.

John Dear, in his reflection on the beatitude of mourning, emphasizes the importance of such empathy. Being empathetic reminds us of our true identity. "Violence starts when we forget who we are, when we forget that we are human beings, sisters and brothers of one another, children of the God of peace." To become mindful of our solidarity with those who suffer, we must make grief a part of our regular spiritual practice. In remembering those who suffer, we "become vulnerable, enter the pain of humanity and creation, and embrace it. In doing so, we grieve with the God who grieves, and weeps. Only then will our hearts be broken and the God of peace console us" (*The Beatitudes of Peace*).

With guidance and grace, we also recognize the presence of God who never abandons us, particularly in our most devastating moments. This makes unthinkable the idea that God willfully rains down suffering upon us or withdraws loved ones from our lives as a spiritual litmus test. "The mystery of personal suffering is not that God permits it, but that God suffers in the loneliness, anguish, and tragic deaths that scream out their denial of a God who cares. In their pain those who suffer call out to the Spirit of Christ in those who hear not the lament of strangers but the heart-rending cry of brothers and sisters.

God's communion with people is never so intense as when human suffering seems to belie the existence of goodness, justice, and hope" (Geffrey B. Kelly, "Sharing in the Pain of God: Dietrich Bonhoeffer's Reflections on Christian Vulnerability," *Weavings*, Vol. VIII, no. 4).

Is this what Aesculus meant by the "awful grace of God"? It is not something that comes without cost: rather, it opens our hearts through the paradoxical process of suffering which yields to awe-filled grace. It also draws us closer to one another as we, like the Emmaus disciples, find solace, support, and solidarity with those who understand not only our pain but also the joy of a re-formed heart.

For Reflection *or* Conversation

How do you experience God in the midst of suffering and loss?

What contributes to a mellowed heart and the purification of memory?

How does the practice of grief enlarge your heart and lead to more compassion and empathy?

Five

The Grace in Grief

When he had said this, as they were looking on, he was lifted up, and a cloud took him from their sight. While they were looking intently at the sky as he was going, suddenly two men dressed in white garments stood beside them. They said, "Men of Galilee, why are you standing there looking at the sky? This Jesus who has been taken up from you into heaven will return in the same way as you have seen him going into heaven." Then they returned to Jerusalem from the mount called Olivet, which is near Jerusalem, a sabbath day's journey away. ACTS 1:9-12

There is something almost humorous in Luke's account of the Ascension and the question posed to the disciples. Even though they witness Jesus being "lifted up" and being taken from their sight, men in white garments—presumably angels—ask why they continue looking into the sky. It's a pressing question about looking in the wrong place for the one who has passed from their sight.

It's also a question posed to anyone who has cause to ponder the whereabouts of someone who has died. Now that humans have journeyed into space, walked on the moon, and sent probes far into the galaxy, the idea of heaven as "up in the sky" becomes increasingly deficient. In a mystical sense, Christ's ascent is not so much vertical as horizontal—a movement into the mystical space in and around us. Thomas Merton described this transcendent reality beautifully: "Life is this simple. We are living in a world that is absolutely transparent, and God is shining through all the time. This is not just a fable or a nice story. It is true. If we abandon ourselves to God and forget ourselves, we see it sometimes, and we see it maybe frequently. God shows Himself everywhere, in everything—in people and in things, in nature and in events. It becomes very obvious that God is everywhere and in everything and we cannot be without Him. It's impossible. The only thing is that we don't see it" (*The Merton Tapes*, "Life and Solitude").

This brings the notion of heaven down to earth in literal fashion. In his book *Learning to Pray*, Wayne Muller writes about a view of heaven from the gospels. "When Jesus described heaven, he never spoke of a place; rather, he described a state of the heart, a way of being attentive to the sacred in ordinary things, things we might easily overlook. He said that if we are awake and present, heaven can be found in such small things like a mustard seed." I once quoted this passage at a retreat, and a woman in the group nearly took my head off. "I refuse to think that my mother isn't in specific *place*," she snapped. I could understand her dismay. It is comforting to think of the deceased resting in an idyllic and cloud-filled space. The tangible is what we know, and so it is natural to cling to an image of heaven as a concrete place where our loved ones now dwell. In this way, we picture them doing their favorite activities as on earth but in a sweetly celestial environment. With more distance, such notions fade as we come to recognize the thin membrane that exists between heaven and earth. When we start looking around us instead of into the sky, grace emerges in unanticipated ways, giving rise to new ways of seeing that in turn generate gratitude, openness, and hope.

THE GRACE OF GRATITUDE

My life goes on in endless song
Above earth's lamentations,
I hear the real, though far-off hymn
That hails a new creation.

Through all the tumult and the strife
I hear its music ringing,
It sounds an echo in my soul.
How can I keep from singing?

ROBERT WADSWORTH LOWRY

("How Can I Keep from Singing?")

As mid-July approaches, I remember my daughter Jenny and my father, Albert, in a particularly visceral way. The anniversaries of their deaths fall two days apart and wrap me in a paradoxical shroud of both grief and gratitude. Since both beloved figures passed out of my life decades ago—first my daughter and then my father—the sharp edges of loss have softened. In place of the immediate anguish and the aftermath of extended sadness comes peace and deep thankfulness for the gift of two wonderful people in my life. This is grief for the long term.

In chapter 1, I described an evolving understanding of grace as something that reverberates in our lives. The long-term process of grief deepens my appreciation for its constant and active nature. John Mogabgab, the former editor of the spiritual journal *Weavings*, wrote about grace as "the continuously and outflowing energy of God's love in which all creatures live and without which we cannot thrive...Grace permits us to see God's luminous purpose shining in creation and grace creates within us the very capacity for such vision" ("Grace Abounding," Editor's Introduction, *Weavings*, Vol. XXIII, no. 1). This is a much more profound view of grace than that of a milky substance that rises and falls according to our good or bad behavior. It speaks of the ongoing reality of God's presence, made present for those with eyes to see and ears to hear. The long road of grief opens grace-filled vistas that allow us to sing in the midst of "tumult and strife" with full and thankful hearts.

The words "grace" and "gratitude" share the same Latin root: *gratia*. Both express mercy, favor, and goodwill. The "awful grace of God" mellows into "awe-filled" grace as we cherish our memories and start to recognize the sacred in each moment. Loss has a way of heightening such awareness by giving us an appreciation of the here and now. Rather than being haphazard, we begin to recognize a stitching together of both our sorrows and our joys. Robert A. Johnson describes these as "slender threads": "Mysterious forces that guide and shape who we are. They are the patterns that give meaning to our experiences." As he continued to reflect upon the accident that nearly took his life as a boy, these threads became more apparent as weaving together all future experiences and learning. "I have gradually learned to accept that the slender threads possess greater intelligence and wisdom than our scrambling egos can ever attain. In good times and bad, one slender thread after another has seen me through and, together, they have shaped what I know and who I am." The tenderness that comes with grief and loss has a way of offering greater receptivity to such self-knowledge.

Heart wounds may not ever completely close, but they also have the potential of becoming receptacles of grace. Melissa M. Kelley describes the wholeness that results from brokenness. "We may come to realize how deeply connected we are. We may come to know that God's abundant love surrounds us and beckons us beyond our grief, into a hopeful future. All of this is gift and grace." Kelley goes on to warn against being glib about such grace, as it comes—particularly for the bereaved—at great cost. "Wholeness doesn't mean our losses cease to hurt…But in everything, God works for good, bringing wholeness out of the brokenness, in love." The one who has known deep heartbreak can appreciate this in a profound way.

My friend Father William McNichols is a renowned iconographer and a deeply spiritual man. Each time he paints an icon, he spends a great deal of time with a sacred figure by reading about his or her life and wisdom. He once told me that on the anniversary of a saint's death, they draw closer to us. Therefore, we celebrate the anniversary of their death as feasts and not somber memorials. It is akin to the way in which Celtic spirituality regards as "thin places" those locales where the distance between earth and heaven dissipates. My recognition of the feasts of Jenny and my father seems to be one of "thin times." For some, there are also experiences of closeness with a deceased loved one through some unexplained phenomenon, through vivid dreams, or through hearing a piece of music. This is a "thin" way of seeing. It is a way of looking, not upward into the sky, but into the grace-filled presence of the sacred all around us.

Such insight can also give rise to an increased awareness and appreciation for generativity. Life goes on "in endless song"—not as a pious platitude but as a vital reality. I am now a grandmother and am moving toward a stage in life where my own death is not that far off. Thus, I give more thought than ever to the legacy I will leave for my grandchildren. This makes looking around instead of up to the heavens an invitation to view what *is* rather than what *was*.

THE GRACE OF OPENNESS

> *Sometimes the particulars of the way in which someone dies, the time, place, even the circumstances, may cause those left behind to wonder whether the event marks the healing of hidden patterns and personal issues, and answers for that person certain lifelong questions. Death has been referred to as the great teacher. It may be the great healer as well.*
>
> RACHEL NAOMI REMEN (Kitchen Table Wisdom)

The month of July recently opened into two more occasions of remembrance. A few days after Jenny's anniversary, I now mark the deaths of two of my sisters. One followed the other in rapid succession, leaving my family shocked and devastated. While I am still in the process of unraveling the aftermath of such a huge loss, I am also reminded that one death or deep loss does nothing to prepare us for another. Grief is grief. Even so, an acquaintance with grief allows us to be patient and to remain open to the grace that can eventually emerge from the wound. It also offers an insight into the value of vulnerability.

Being vulnerable tends to be associated with weakness and inferiority—something to be overcome rather than yielded to. Personal and national security is seen as the ideal, even if it is mostly illusory. This can be one way we close off after a time of loss: afraid to open ourselves to a loving relationship lest we suffer another devastating loss. In truth, vulnerability can bridge the gap between isolation out of fear or self-defensiveness to solidarity with others and a sharing in our common humanity. "Properly understood...the term describes the fundamental openness of the human being to be affected by life, persons, and events. To be human is to be vulnerable, indeed defenseless, in the face of so many of the events and persons that touch us, for good or ill. At the most fundamental level, human vulnerability is part and parcel of being a person, having a body, being embodied" (Michael Downey, "Brief Gold," *Weavings*, Vol. VIII, no. 4).

Being vulnerable offers an opening into relationships and communion with others who recognize their own weakness and pain. Sorrow has a particular way of generating deeper connections as we allow our own vulnerability to touch that in another. The seeds of the divine and capacities of the human heart are found not in strength but in weakness. When we remain open-hearted, grief gives us the capacity to empathize and to offer genuine support and comfort to others. We also gain a capacity for insight and reflection that generates a broader perspective.

As devastating as it was to lose all three of my sisters within the span of eighteen months, I also saw the grace within the timing of their deaths. Due to various physical frailties, all three would have been particularly susceptible to the dangers of the Covid-19 virus, and the pandemic restrictions would have isolated them from other members of the family. I mentioned in an earlier chapter how grateful I was that Jenny died at home and not in a hospital bed. Through these losses I am able to see patterns of grace that, as Rachel Naomi Remen notes, are part of death's potential to bring healing.

I once read that if our society regarded death as more of a question mark than a period, we would view it quite differently. While it is a great mystery, it is also the one certainty in life: we are all going to die. In addition, death offers opportunities to live well. John O'Donohue calls them an invitation to embrace openness and serenity. "To practice this art of being is to come into your soul-rhythm...Then the final meeting with your physical death need not be threatening or destructive. That final meeting will be the encounter with your own deepest identity, namely, your soul" (*Anam Cara: A Book of Celtic Wisdom*). The long path of grief can free us from our own fears around death and provide an opening into hope.

THE GRACE OF HOPE

But all will be well, and all will be well,
and all manner of thing will be well.

JULIAN OF NORWICH

I became acquainted with grief at a very young age. My mother never shied from acknowledging deaths in our family. Most post-funeral meals took place at our home and were occasions for storytelling and the sharing of memory. I saw a dead person for the first time when Mom took me with her to the Rosary offered for her Aunt Jo. I was only six or seven years old, but I vividly remember viewing the body in an open coffin. A few years later, my cousin was killed in a tragic car accident while on her honeymoon. I can still recall seeing her in the casket dressed in her wedding gown. Both experiences—far apart in terms of terms of their impact on our family—gave me an initial recognition of both the natural passing of a person at the end of a long life and the tragic occurrences that can end a life prematurely.

I look back at these experiences with gratitude. My mother was part of a generation for whom death was a constant reality. She lived through two world wars as well as the Spanish flu epidemic. While quite young during the latter, she no doubt became aware of the mourning that took place around her. She once told me how she and a cousin mimicked the funeral of an uncle by carrying an empty carton somberly around the house. As an adult she was mortified by how it must have looked to her grieving aunt. I found it revelatory. She learned at an early age that death was a natural part of life and imparted the same understanding to me.

My youthful experience of attending funerals and sharing stories made death less daunting and seeded a recognition of grief as a process threaded with both sorrow and hope. The latter arises when we realize that our heart wounds needn't be fatal. As Henri Nouwen observed, "When we become aware that we do not have to escape our pains, but that we can mobilize them into a common search for life, those very pains are transformed from expressions of despair into signs of hope" (from the introduction to *Wounded Healers*, quoted in *Weavings*, Vol. XIII, no. 5).

Of the three theological virtues, hope may be the least understood. It is easily confused with optimism, wishful thinking, or even hopelessness. After all, if a doctor told you, "There is nothing to do now but hope," you would know your days are numbered. Therefore, when I consider hope, I turn to the familiar quote from Julian of Norwich. We might dismiss her view of "all will be well" as pious or simplistic until we stop to consider the context of her life. She survived a serious illness that brought her to death's doorstep. She lived through the Black Death and the Peasants' Revolt—events which made suffering and death a backdrop to her revelations. Because we know so little about her personal life, it may well be that she experienced the loss of loved ones because of one of these tragic events. When her visions (called "showings") revealed that "all manner of thing" would be well, there were no time parameters placed around it. There was no proviso for all being well in the next day or year or even in her lifetime. Hope trusts in the long view and in an underlying recognition and embrace of grace. It becomes one of those slender threads that weaves meaning into and makes sense out of some of the deepest experiences of grief and loss.

For Reflection *or* Conversation

How do you envision heaven?

What gratitude or openness has arisen in you during a time of grief?

How do you find hope in the midst of grief?

SACRED THREADS

After asking about a picture of Jenny on my bookshelf, my three-year-old granddaughter told me, "I remember her." I wondered: Was it an association with a baby who resembled her or a pre-birth memory? Either way, I saw it as a slender thread running from Jenny's life and into that of her young niece. In a larger sense, I see it as part of the cosmic threads that draw everything together in a tapestry of sacred unity. This is the essence of grace—the great weaving together of all that was and is and will be. "Grace is what God does to keep all things God has made in love and alive—forever" (Richard Rohr).

When I try to picture where Jenny—along with my mother and father, my sisters, and other loved ones—now dwells, the best I can imagine is the river that flows very close to our home. Just as one drop of water cannot be singled out, neither can the souls that flow together in the great river of Divine love. In the same way, each drop adds to the flow and beauty of the river. This is what heaven has come to mean to me. It is not something far off and attainable only after we have lived suitable moral lives: it is accessible here and now as well as beyond the here and now. As Catherine of Siena described it, "All the way to heaven is heaven."

This is not a recognition I could have reached in the immediate days or even years after Jenny's death. It didn't awaken in the blink of an eye but in a slow, unfolding fashion. Along with it comes the gratitude arising from grace in a wound that will never entirely close. This emerges in my final letter to Jenny:

Thank you, Jenny, for all that you taught me—about weakness and true strength, about patience, about loving and caring, about the power of one life to affect another's as yours did mine. Our lives continue to be intertwined, and though I still look forward to that sweet reunion with you, I feel better able to wait a while.

While I attributed that inner knowledge to Jenny, I now view it as the lesson that comes from accumulated grief—that which I experienced through the large and small losses taking place throughout the intervening years. Like those long-ago disciples, I stopped looking up into another space for what exists all around me—the presence of Divine Love that permeates everything. In sharing a bit of my story, I hope that you, dear reader, have unspooled a bit more of your own and, in doing so, recognize the grace that is threaded within and beyond the losses that have reshaped your heart.

For Reflection *or* Conversation

What knowledge have you attained through accumulated grief?

What sacred thread has woven through your life?

How have you discovered grace in the wound?

Resources

BOOKS

Dear, John. *The Beatitudes of Peace* (Twenty-Third Publications, 2016)

Felice, Margaret. *Helping Teens with Grief* (Twenty-Third Publications, 2023)

Finley, James. *Christian Meditation: Experiencing the Presence of God* (HarperOne, 2005)

Flinders, Carol Lee. *Enduring Grace: Living Portraits of Seven Women Mystics* (HarperCollins, 1993)

Hart, Thomas. *Spiritual Quest: A Guide to the Spiritual Landscape* (Paulist Press, 1999)

Johnson, Robert A. *Balancing Heaven and Earth* (HarperOne, 1998)

Kelley, Melissa M. *Grief: Contemporary Theory and the Practice of Ministry* (Fortress Press, 2010)

Lamott, Anne. *Grace (Eventually): Thoughts on Faith* (Riverhead Books, 2007)

Lewis, C.S. *A Grief Observed* (HarperOne, 2015)

Resources

Lindbergh, Anne Morrow. *Hour of Gold, Hour of Lead: Diaries and Letters of Anne Morrow Lindbergh* (Mariner Books, 1993)

Mairs, Nancy. *Ordinary Time: Cycles in Marriage, Faith, and Renewal* (Beacon Press, 1993)

Moskowitz, Fran. *A Leak in the Heart: Tales from a Woman's Heart* (David R. Godine, 1985)

Muller, Wayne. *Learning to Pray: How We Find Heaven on Earth* (Bantam Books, 2003)

Nouwen, Henri. *The Road to Daybreak: A Spiritual Journey* (Image, 1990)

O'Donohue, John. *Anam Cara: A Book of Celtic Wisdom* (HarperCollins, 1997)

Paulus, Trina. *Hope for the Flowers* (Newman Press, 1972)

Remen, Rachel Naomi. *Kitchen Table Wisdom: Stories that Heal* (Riverhead Books, 1997)

Starr, Mirabai. *Caravan of No Despair: A Memoir of Loss and Transformation* (Sounds True, 2015)

Periodicals and Websites

Beloved Sons Series: Men and Grief CD by Richard Rohr. Available through the Center for Action and Contemplation bookstore: www.cac.org

Center for Action and Contemplation. Daily meditations offered by Father Richard Rohr and others. www.Meditations@cac.org

Gratefulness. A website sponsored by the Network for Grateful Living: www.gratefulness.org.

Still Blooming: www.stillblooming.blog. A website created by my friend and colleague Barbara Radtke and me.

The Thomas Merton Center at Bellarmine University: www.merton.org. Contains a comprehensive collection of Merton's writings as well as access to his audio recordings.

Weavings: A Journal of the Spiritual Life. The Upper Room: www.upperroom.org. [Note: This wonderful publication went out of print in 2017. I still have years' worth of back issues and draw upon the wisdom of the authors for insights into various spiritual topics. I hope the reader will explore the works of the authors I have included in the book for further inspiration.]

William Hart McNichols Art Shop. Official website of Father Bill's icons and containing his blogs: https://frbillmcnichols-sacredimages.com.